INSOMNIA
MY
WAKE UP
CALL

BEV DIEMLER

He is with us!!!

Bev

Cover design by Jayson R. Buenaagua

ISBN: 0692312005
ISBN-13: 978-0692312001

CONTENTS

dedication

I dedicate this book to my husband, Steve Diemler, whose prayers brought about my conversion, and subsequently, this little book.

.

acknowledgments

I've known I was supposed to write this book for over ten years. However, I didn't believe I could really do it. In an attempt to avoid writing the book, I tried my hand at blogging it first. My dear friend and brother in Christ, Jayson R. Buenaagua read my first incomplete attempt at recording my conversion experience. He believed that I should actually write the book so much so, that on Christmas Eve, 2012, he designed the cover and gave it to me as a gift. Thank you from the bottom of my heart for the little push I needed to take that leap of faith. I will always cherish our friendship as well as the beautiful cover you created. It really is perfect.

I also want to thank Julie Gubash and Ophelia Umunna, who believed in me from the beginning and supported me every step of the way.

I am so blessed to be able to call Dr. Thomas Loome, my friend. I will never be able to thank you enough for critiquing that first draft in your gentle, honest way. You validated my story and your words are directly responsible for my pursuing getting it published. Thank you so much.

Most of all, I want to acknowledge my family for always being proud of me and believing in me, no matter what I do or how crazy it seems. I love you guys.

introduction

I am writing this journal for anyone, and everyone who has ever gone to bed tired and fallen asleep, only to wake up and toss and turn and watch the clock change, hour after hour, all through the night, until they finally fall asleep, right before the alarm goes off.

I know it well. I had insomnia almost every night for a year. You know how some people say everything happens for a reason? Well, insomnia changed my life. I would go so far as to say, insomnia saved my life. This is my story.

one

I am a very ordinary person. I've lived a pretty typical, uneventful life. There is nothing special or different about me. If I had to describe myself, I would say that I am one of those people who like to be busy. The busier I am, the happier I am.

My story starts at a point in my life when I was extremely happy. Life was good. I was happy because I was busy, and I was busy because my house was full of children. Children have always been what I enjoyed more than anything.

I was running a daycare out of my home. My husband and I were also foster parents and, we had just had our very own baby girl. Also, my youngest son, Joey, was still at home, and even though his two older brothers had moved out to start their own lives, they lived in town and were around a lot.

It was such a happy and rewarding time. I felt like I had really become my own person, and I was comfortable with who I had become. I was doing something worthwhile with my life...finally. I wasn't just surviving. I was making a difference. At that time, I loved everything about my life.

Before that, things hadn't always been so good for me. My happy childhood had ended with divorce. Both of my parents became alcoholics. I ran away when I was seventeen, then, I entered into a loveless, abusive marriage that lasted fifteen years.

The only good thing that came out of that time in my life was my three boys. I lived for them. They were all I cared about. When I finally got out, all I wanted was to be alone with my boys, in peace. I thought life couldn't get any better. Then, I met Steve. I suddenly became Cinderella. I never really thought I could live happily ever after, in love, (I had never really been in love before) but, there I was. That is, until we tried to have a child of our own. That's when, sorrow entered my life again. I had three miscarriages, and then, our perfect little girl was stillborn.

We were devastated. After we buried our baby, Hannah Leigh, I gave up. I gave up on ever having a child with the love of my life, on ever having a little girl, and on me and Steve ever starting our own family because we didn't want to adopt. It was a really sad time.

I kept busy with work and tried not to dwell on things. Then one day, I heard about foster care for the first time. There was an article in a Kansas City paper about a family's pet ferret practically eating a baby alive while she slept in-between her parents. They had passed out from "drinking beer" they said. It just made me sick to think about it. It went on to say the baby was recovering and in foster care.

I didn't know what foster care was but, I remember thinking that I could take care of that baby girl. I started checking into it and that is when we decided to become foster parents. I thought if we couldn't have a child of our own, at least we could help and love children that were in need. It is still one of the best decisions we ever made.

We went to work on getting licensed and becoming official foster parents. I think it took us about six months. However, it only took a few days to get foster kids after we were licensed. The first week we were given a two-year-old boy. The next week, we were given a one-year-old little boy. It was so amazing to have toddlers in the house. I can't really explain how rewarding it is to know you were doing something so important for a needy child. Maybe I had made a difference in someone else's life before, I don't know, but this felt like the most important thing I had ever done and I loved it. Being a foster mom felt like a calling to me.

I soon found out foster care has its ups and its downs, too. The second little boy was sent back to his mother. She was not supposed to have him but, because she crossed the county line, the new county didn't acknowledge the court order. They gave him back. It was terrible. I was so upset. I felt their politics were coming ahead of his safety and well-being.

While explaining all of this to my daycare lady the next afternoon, she told me about a baby girl she had that was also in foster care. The mom was an emergency foster care provider, which meant she was only supposed to have them until they could be placed in a more permanent home. She said this mom was getting very upset because she had been there for over two weeks.

My radar had gone up at the mention of a girl and then she took me in the baby's room to see her. I'll never forget the first time we saw each other. She was so cute. She had these big brown eyes and she smiled at me as if she wanted me to pick her up. I fell in love. The daycare owner actually orchestrated the switch. I never met her worker until after she had come home with me. I was somewhat afraid to take her home the first night because there should have been an official person to do the hand off and give me the paperwork. I did finally talk to someone on the phone and they said take her.

It was late and the other foster mom hadn't come to pick her up so, I took her home. I couldn't understand how her mom and the other lady didn't want her. I would have almost killed someone to have an adorable baby girl like her. It is still a mystery to me, to this day.

It seems like my life can never be all good or all bad. It is always a mixture of both. As happy as I was about getting to bring that baby girl home, I was also upset because I had found out that I was pregnant again. You would think someone who wanted a baby as much as I did would be happy but, I wasn't. After Hannah, I was convinced I would never carry a baby to term. I was not looking forward to another loss and another miscarriage. We were done with it. That is why we had become foster parents. And to top it off, Steve and I were not on the same page about the pregnancy. He thought I should take it easy and get plenty of rest and things might work out this time. I knew they wouldn't. I don't know how we always seem to end up exactly opposite of each other and still make our marriage work but we do.

He was still grieving for our baby. He had also changed jobs before we got married. Life was very stressful and our foster parenting had started off faster than either one of us had expected. He wanted me to slow down. I really had to work hard to convince him to let me bring Big Brown Eyes home. It was only supposed to be for a couple of weeks and he knew how badly I wanted to do it so, he finally agreed.

I am not the only one who fell in love with that pretty baby girl. The minute I got home from work with the kids and my son, Joey, got home from football practice, she was the main attraction. Joey and I spent so many hours teaching her how to walk back and forth between us. We would take her to my work to show everyone what we had taught her. Naturally, she wouldn't show them anything we wanted her to.

My big boys were excited about all of the changes, too. She was also growing on Steve and he was spending more and more time with her and the other little boy, who really liked her, as well. It seemed like she just sort of waltzed in and took over our happy little home. And she did.

On the surface, it seemed like all was good. I kept my pregnancy a secret because I thought I would die if one more person looked at me as if they felt sorry for me. Then it happened. On Christmas Eve, I started spotting. I couldn't believe the timing. A miscarriage on Christmas! Really! Steve insisted I go to bed. He took the kids to the Christmas Eve Mass.

I laid in bed, madder than hell and he went to church and prayed like hell. Long story short, my spotting stopped. I never had the miscarriage I was expecting. I never allowed myself the joy of expecting a beautiful baby until about the seventh month. I kept on waiting for the tragedy but, it never happened. That's right! It never happened. I took those kids to daycare and went to work every day as though nothing had changed. But, in the back of my mind, I held my breath waiting for the day I would have to hold another beautiful baby girl who looked like her daddy and wasn't breathing and had turned purple. Sometimes, I still can't believe it didn't happen.

The brokenhearted woman, who thought she would never have a baby girl of her own, experienced a miracle. Not only did she give birth to a perfect little girl, she also had the opportunity to adopt the other little girl she had fallen in love with. I'm telling you, it just doesn't get much better than that. But, for me, it did get better. My oldest son and his wife had a little baby girl, too. That brings me back to the beginning of my story.

I was in heaven. I had my Katie and I had my Courtney, whom we had adopted. And then, I had my granddaughter, Sadie, too. I quit my job and opened a daycare in my home. I cared for four to six children, Monday through Friday, plus my four foster children. I loved being a mother and a grandmother more than anything else. I was completely happy.

My life was perfect. I had so much more than I had ever expected or ever even dreamed of. I was head over heels in love with my three girls and four adorable little toddlers who came over to play with them each week. I was making pretty good money doing what I loved. Life was so rich and then, I had the foster parent thing, too. I cannot even begin to tell you what it feels like to get a phone call and to hear that the police have just arrested someone and that they have a three-month-old baby that needs a place to stay. It's a mixture of adrenaline and tears. They bring you a scared, usually dirty and always hungry little baby. I was always, somehow, able to bond with those babies and calm their fears. I knew I had a gift.

I would clean them up, feed them, rock them, and sing to them. They would settle down and go to sleep. And then, right before my eyes, they were transformed from scared, hungry, sad little kids, into happy, laughing, normal little angels.

My life had meaning and purpose. I had found something I was good at, something that mattered. I felt fulfilled and rewarded. It really did seem perfect to me. I would get up at five a.m. jog five miles, come home and shower and then start making bottles and Sippy cups. I would get my kids up and ready for the other kids who were being dropped off. I really couldn't imagine my life ever being better than this. I was happier than I had ever been. That is, until the day my husband came home from work and told me his company was transferring him/us to Minnesota.

two

You know, I love children and I love being busy. Let me tell you what I hate. I hate being away from my kids and I hate being cold. I never took my first son, Hurley, to a babysitter. I only took the two boys to one after Willie was almost one and I knew that I was going to eventually get a divorce and be on my own. I never found a sitter I was happy with so, I quit working and opened a daycare in my home. I made more money doing that anyway.

When they were old enough to go to school, I went back to work but, with my Katie, I just couldn't. That is why I started another daycare after she was born. I loved being with my kids all the time. I still do. And the cold... you can have it. I HATE winter. I freeze. I sleep in socks year round because my feet are always cold. I like to wear long sleeves and even sweaters in the summer. I loved having a waterbed because I could keep it like an oven.

The worst kind of cold for me is the wind. Cold

winds go right through me and once I start shivering, it takes a long time to warm me up. Immediately after Steve dropped the bomb, I turned on the Weather Channel. There was a woman about to be blown over by a freezing wind. She was in Minneapolis doing a forecast outside. I couldn't believe it! Me in, Minnesota was the worst possible nightmare I could imagine. What about my boys? What about my foster kids? What about my daycare kids? What about my granddaughter? What about Joey graduating from high school? What about how much I HATE THE COLD?

We weighed all of our options. We were going to have to move. There was no getting around it. Steve had invested too much time training for this new job to quit and start over somewhere else.

There were so many things to do. We had to sell our home. We decided to let Joey stay behind and live with his older brother so he could finish school. He wanted to graduate with his friends. Finding new foster homes for the kids took a lot of time because there was always a shortage of foster homes.

I did find someone to adopt the little girl I had for a year. That felt good. I closed the daycare. We got an offer on our house in three weeks. Steve went ahead. I stayed behind with the girls to close on the house and hire a moving company. Everything was falling into place. We were also going to be fortunate enough to move to Minnesota in January, the coldest month of the year.

Finally the time came for us to move. I had moved about twenty times in the past but this was the first time I ever had the luxury of having a moving company. They came in, packed everything and loaded it. I highly recommend it. When the house was empty, we went to a hotel. The boys came over and hung out with us for our last night in town.

I didn't expect to be as sad as I was. I ended up crying all night and barely slept. I went to the house one last time and loaded up my dog and Steve's cat. Then, I went to the realtor to sign all the paper work and just like that, the happiest time of my life ended.

Steve gave me directions for a shortcut, which was supposed to make us get there in eight hours instead of nine or ten. My state of mind and lack of sleep did not make for the best driving experience. I got lost around Des Moines and it ended up taking us eleven hours to get to our new place in Minnesota. It was awful.

The cat meowed all the way to Iowa until I finally let him out of his cage. Courtney had a new Barbie doll. It sang a horrible song repeatedly for eleven hours. I felt as if my heart would break. We arrived before our furniture. Steve was waiting for us with a couple of air mattresses and sleeping bags in a cabin he had rented for six months on a lake.

Winter in Minnesota is not anything like winter in Missouri. The lakes freeze over up here and people make little towns out on the ice. There are fish houses, trucks and snowmobiles everywhere. It was like a different world. The adventure of it all helped keep me from getting too depressed.

The movers showed up. We were able to fit

everything in the tiny cabin. We were only going to stay in the cabin for six months while we looked for a house to buy. We didn't unpack anything we didn't have to. After the movers left, Steve ordered pizza. I ran up to the gas station to get a six-pack of beer. I found out that they don't sell beer at the gas stations or grocery stores in Minnesota. I couldn't believe it. You have to make a special trip into town to a "liquor store" if you want anything with alcohol. What! It was at that moment that I knew I was not going to like this new place at all. Not only was it ungodly cold, it was also STUPID!

three

i've told you how my life always seems to have good mixed in with the bad and vice versa. Well, our move up north was no different. Steve's sister and her husband and two children had moved to Minnesota a few years before us. The cabin Steve had rented, was in the town where they lived. We were not going to be alone up here. We were going to have family to visit with.

We survived our first Friday night on the lake with delivered pizza and no beer. On Saturday morning, I heard the strangest sound outside. It was a cross between a weed eater, a chainsaw and a motorcycle. We ran to the window and there were two snowmobiles going around the house. It was Steve's brother-in-law and his son. They had ridden their sleds through town, across the lake and up to our front door. It was beginning to look like we might have some fun in Minnesota, after all.

Steve had a snowmobile by the next Saturday and we started spending most weekends together. I had only met them briefly, a couple of times in the past but, I liked them right off the bat. We all got along so well and had so much fun. It really did take the sting out of our move.

We started settling in and adjusting to the winter-wonderland. Steve's brother-in-law set up his fish house on our lake. We all got to check out ice fishing. I learned how to ride the snowmobile so I could take the girls for rides during the day. We had tried to clear an area on the lake so the girls could ice-skate, that is until we got 36 inches of snow one day. It was my first white out and it was creepy.

One good thing about being in the cabin all day with only the two little girls was that I could really devote myself to them. We played dress up and with the dollhouses. Steve brought home a new little kitten. I wasn't going a hundred miles an hour anymore taking care of a ton of kids but, I still kept busy. It allowed me time to do some things I really enjoyed, like crocheting and quilting.

All of the boys came up, along with my granddaughter and it was great. They got to experience frozen lake life before the thaw. All in all, we were doing pretty well.

Being home with the girls all day and spending time with the in-laws on the weekends was wonderful but, whenever I left the house, I hated it. Everywhere I went, I ran into rude people. I hated the grocery store and the gas station. I really hated the liquor store. I could stay upset about each trip out for days. I was always complaining to Steve's sister and brother-in-law about how rude people were. They couldn't understand it, though. They seemed to like everyone. They thought the people in the stores were nice. They said they didn't get how I could not like it. I couldn't really explain it to them, either. Then one day I heard the phrase *Minnesota Nice.*

I remember thinking that the people up here were so arrogant that they had to give a name to their niceness. It seemed like bragging to me and what was worse, I thought it was totally hypocritical. I decided the saying, *Minnesota Nice,* was an oxymoron.

four

We made a plan before we moved that would give us plenty of time to find a fantastic house in the best area of the Twin Cities. We all came up around Thanksgiving and spent two days driving through all of the suburbs to see which one we liked best. Hands down, we all loved White Bear Lake.

Then Steve rented a cabin for six months in Forest Lake, where his sister lived, so we could take our time while we house hunted. When we moved here, it was a very strange time in the Real Estate market. There were not many houses listed to look at and the ones that were listed, went fast. Sometimes they even went for over the asking price. The prices of the homes were crazy, too. We had sold a beautiful 3-bedroom home in Missouri for a little over $100,000. When we got here, the houses in that range were such dumps that we wouldn't even consider looking at them. The houses we would consider living in were way out of our budget.

We had seen everything in White Bear Lake without any possibilities and we were already at four months and started to panic. Our plan wasn't working out. We couldn't extend our lease. The property owner had promised our place to her son and his friends when they got out of college that spring. We decided we should start looking in Forest Lake. I hated it but, we needed something.

My husband had decided to become religious after we started dating. It drove me nuts but I was in love. He had gotten me to agree to get married in a Catholic Church. I did because it was so important to him. I had to get my first marriage annulled. That was a nightmare. Moreover, I had agreed any children would go to Catholic School. I wanted to make him happy. I believe part of that agreement was that I would not have to have anything to do with it, because I hated school and I hated anything religious.

When we decided to look in Forest Lake, the first thing we had to do was look at the Catholic School. We got there with the girls and found signs on all of the doors warning of an outbreak of head lice. Immediately, I hated that school as much as I hated where we were living. Now, we were really in panic mode.

Steve took off early one afternoon. He said wanted to drive to Stillwater, to look at it. We were also considering Hudson, Wisconsin. Stillwater was a cute little town. It was on a river instead of a lake and it had a lift bridge. It seemed somewhat charming. We drove up the hill from downtown and saw a big Catholic Church with a school attached.

Steve parked and we took the girls inside.

The woman who showed us around said that they always had a waiting list and that the people with children already enrolled got first pick. Surprisingly though, there wasn't a wait when we were there. We looked at the church; we decided right on the spot it was where we wanted our Courtney. We gave them a deposit to hold her place, then we went to the car and called our realtor and told him to start looking in Stillwater.

It only took a few days to see everything in Stillwater. I would go on line several times a day to see if there was anything new. One day I saw an old Victorian house. I did a drive by first, and it wasn't too bad. I called Steve and he said to set something up for Saturday. I did and when we looked at the house, I fell in love with it. It was so Victorian. It also had a swimming pool and hot tub. The kitchen had glass doors on the cabinets so you could see the dishes. It had an awesome fireplace and it even had an attic fan. We had one in our first house and loved it. It was perfect. It was even within walking distance of the school and church. However, something about the house made Steve nervous. He wasn't sold.

We had started going to church in Stillwater on Sundays so, we drove by the house again after church, trying to decide what to do. We were out of time and any house was going to sell right away with the market the way it was. We drove around a bit and suddenly spotted a big old house on a corner with a little for sale by owner sign. I jumped out and grabbed a flyer. It was going to be open in a couple of hours. We could look at it without setting up an appointment and time was of the essence. Steve and the girls were tired and hungry so we drove back to Forest Lake. He talked me into driving back and looking at it later.

I drove back by myself and looked at the house. I immediately didn't like it but, I was convinced that if Steve saw it, he would realize that the other house was the one for us. We needed to hurry up and make an offer. They were going to have another open house on Thursday. Steve said he would drive over after work and check it out. I spent the week shopping for new Blue Willow dishes that would look awesome in the glass cabinets of the Victorian house. I knew we would be buying it as soon as Steve saw the other house. I believe I went shopping for curtains, too.

I don't know why things can't ever seem to go according to my plans but, they don't. When Steve came home, he had a weird, very weird, look on his face. He proceeded to tell me he loved the house. He said he loved it so much that he didn't want to leave. He said he had never felt so comfortable in a home. He was more convinced than ever that the Victorian would be a mistake. He said he even wanted to make an offer on this house right on the spot! So began the love/hate relationship with the house that would eventually become our new home.

After much negotiation and many twists and turns, we moved into our new home on August 15, 2003. We had barely gotten settled when Courtney started kindergarten.

five

So began, what my precious Katie, refers to as "the good ole days." The "good ole days" were when it was only the two of us, Katie and me. We would walk Courtney to school and then for the first time since she had been born, we were alone for the day. I will never be able to put into words what Katie meant to me. She was absolutely the most beautiful, sweet, precious little girl who had ever been born. Moreover, she loved me almost as much as I loved her. I was the one that she wanted to hold her. I was the one she would talk to. We were made for each other.

Every time we went somewhere in the car, she would reach up to the front seat and hold my hand and say, she loved me over and over again. There has never been a more perfect daughter in the entire world. There just couldn't be. She was so much more than I could have ever even dreamed of. I felt like the luckiest, most undeserving woman on the face of the earth. To have a little girl like her and

21

then to have another little girl I loved so much, too, was surreal, especially after three boys. Then to top it off, I had the most wonderful husband in the world. I was living in a dream. I missed my boys and my old life but those little girls made everything okay. The icing on the cake was when my Joey graduated and moved up to be with us. He got a job at Andersen Windows. Life was good. I really felt so complete having my youngest son back home again.

The recurring theme of my life, you know, can't seem to have good without the bad, was determined to hang around. I had been forced to leave what I thought was the best time of my life and start over again, in a place I hated, in the cold and away from my boys but, I had done it. I had done it well. I was in a really good place and happy again. The "good ole days" as my sweet baby girl called them, were turning into the happiest time of my life, that is, until I started having insomnia.

Now, I have had insomnia in the past from time to time, like most people, but it had never been a real problem. This insomnia, however, was different. Every night, I would go to sleep and then, after a couple of hours or more, I would wake up and not be able to go back to sleep for the rest of the night. It actually felt like I fell asleep right before the alarm went off, every morning. Night after night, lying awake, watching the hours tick away became my sleeping habit.

I started taking a Tylenol pm… same thing would happen. I started taking two… same thing would happen. I added a glass of wine but, I would still wake up in the wee hours of the morning and not be able to go back to sleep. The pills and the wine were making me fall asleep really good, pass out even. But, they didn't keep me asleep. I was still waking up and laying there fully conscious, every night.

Insomnia was becoming my reality and I didn't like it. In the beginning, I would spend most of my non-sleeping time being irritated and trying to fall back asleep. Then my bad temper would kick in and I would spend most of the nights angry.

I've always believed in karma so I would occupy myself with wondering what I had done or was doing wrong to be making this happen. Of course, it had to be my fault, right. What goes around comes around was my mantra. I worked very hard at not having negative thoughts so I wouldn't have to have them return to me. Whenever I got upset, I would try to get rid of those thoughts with music or noise of some kind. When I couldn't stop them, I would use heavy metal music to drown them out and it worked great. Who can think when that noise is blaring!

After several months of insomnia, I began to realize there was more going on than just my inability to sleep. As I lay there awake, night after night, I discovered that in addition to being irritated and tired, I was also sad. That is putting it lightly. I felt as if I was being swallowed up in sadness. I would lay there, in-between the two little girls that had made me that happiest woman in the world, and suddenly become so overwhelmed with sadness, that I felt like I was going to die.

At first, I tried to rationalize the feeling engulfing me. I had been sad when I had to move. I missed my boys and my granddaughter. I missed my old house. I was part owner of a house I didn't like that much. Of course, I would naturally be a little down, right. However, everything about this was different.

I wasn't just a little depressed. I was more than depressed. The best way I can put it into words is to say that I felt empty. My insomnia was now not so much about being awake when I wanted to sleep. It was about the emptiness. It seemed like I was sadder than I had ever been in my entire life. It was worse than when I realized I was in labor too early or when I had to bury my baby girl or when we were forced to move to the coldest state in the Union. I felt like I had a hole in my heart. Something was missing.

What was going on with me? During the day, I was living the "good ole days" with my Katie and during the night, I was drowning in despair. It just didn't make sense. I know depression, okay. I almost had a nervous breakdown when I ran away from home. I was homeless more than once. I married a man I didn't love to get off of the street. I watched my husband become an alcoholic in front of his adorable little boys. I was a single mom who couldn't make ends meet. I had many days when I didn't want to get out of bed or answer the phone because of the bill collector's calls.

I had to warm water in the microwave to give my boys a bath when I didn't have money to fill the propane tank. I know what hard times are and what depression feels like. But, what I was experiencing with the insomnia was so much worse. I think what made it worse was that I didn't have anything or any reason to feel empty and alone.

I liked to say Minnesota Nice was an oxymoron. Now I was becoming an oxymoron! Damn Karma. How was it possible to be so happy during the day and so miserable at night? It was at that time I started beating myself up every night, as I laid awake. I would play this little game where I would go through my life and remember how bad things had been and how good they were now.

I would go through all of the scenarios of how situations could have ended up terrible. Yet they always ended up better than I could have ever imagined. I think I was trying to prove to myself that I didn't have anything to be sad about, even though I already knew that. I started self-loathing. What was wrong with me? I had no reason to feel empty and lonely so, why was I? Nothing worked. No matter how hard I tried, I couldn't get rid of the insomnia or the big black hole that I was visiting each night.

Years ago, I realized that the only person who was ever going to help me, was myself. That is when I discovered the section in the bookstore called "Self-help" books. The most influential book I had ever read was a book I picked up by Dr. Wayne Dyer called "Your Erroneous Zones". I have to tell you, I feel like that book changed my life.

I learned I had lived my whole life as a victim. I was one of those people who blamed the way I felt on other people. He made me angry, and she hurt my feelings were my go-to phrases. When I read Your Erroneous Zones, I began to understand that I was the only one responsible for how I felt and how I reacted to anything.

His little book explained my life. I learned how I reacted to anything was my choice. That little book was not only life changing, it was empowering. I went from "He made me angry." and "He hurt my feelings." to "You are an idiot and what you say about me doesn't even matter because I don't care what you think." I turned into an unhurt-able bad ass that began to take responsibility for how I felt and what I did. It was reading that little book that helped me know I was strong enough to make a life for my boys and myself. I filed for divorce. I began to believe how I felt was my choice, so much so, that I blamed everything in my life that I didn't like, only on me.

I knew, deep down in my soul, that if I was feeling unhappy or sad, it was no one's fault but my own. If I felt empty and lonely, it was because I was choosing to feel that way. I admit it is embarrassing to realize you have been choosing to be a victim or even worse, you have been choosing to feel sorry for yourself. But, it is truly what I believed. How we felt was up to us.

So, the overwhelming sadness I was experiencing and the total emptiness had to be what I wanted. The only thing I couldn't figure out was why. Why would I want to be so sad when I had more to be happy about than I had ever had in my entire life? What was wrong with me? I didn't know. The only thing I could come up with was that

I must have been going crazy. It was that moment when I realized that perhaps, I needed some help.

six

i needed help. That meant I needed a new self-help book. I made a mental note that morning to go to Barnes and Noble over the weekend so I could put an end to my insomnia insanity. Steve was in Chicago, again, at school and after the girls had dinner, we ran over to Walmart to pick something up. I caught their small little book/magazine section out of the corner of my eye on our way to check out so, we walked over to see what they had.

Voila! A miracle happened. On the shelf was a little, literally little, book by none other than Dr. Wayne Dyer. The title was *Ten Secrets to Success and Inner Peace*. The words Inner Peace weren't really in my vocabulary but, the instant I read them on that book, I knew that Inner Peace was what I needed. Talk about easy! I bought it, went home, got the girls in bed and then read the entire book.

Once again, the good and the bad thing were present. I cannot remember ever reading anything about God in his first book that had changed my life but, he mentioned God quite a bit in this book. I had a problem with any talk of God. I hated it and wouldn't tolerate it but, I was in dire need of help and I really thought this Inner Peace thing was what I needed so, I ignored the God stuff and kept reading.

I really believed in Dr. Dyer because of how much he had helped me in the past so, I just read it. I skipped over what I didn't like and took away from it, two little gems. The first one was *you cannot let your music die in you.* For me, it meant, I needed to be doing what I was called to do. I knew my calling was to be a foster mom. Not doing it was perhaps why I was feeling empty.

I had contacted the county once we were settled, to see about being foster parents again and they had told me there was no need and if I did become a foster parent, I would never, ever get any babies. I would only get teenagers. I had said thanks but, no thanks. Now, I knew I needed to go ahead and get licensed and see what happened. At least I would be ready in the event they ever needed someone to take care of a baby. I was beginning to feel better already.

The second gem was this... *you need to have some silence in your life each and every day or you will not be able to have inner peace.* I couldn't believe it. Silence? Really? I spent my days making sure I didn't have any silence. It was nonexistent in my daily schedule. The TV was on or the radio or the CD player. I avoided silence like the plague. Silence was a scary concept for me. I didn't like it.

I was desperate for a way to end the unbearable

insomnia and emptiness that I was experiencing every night, so I made up my mind that every single day, starting tomorrow, I would turn everything off and observe a moment of silence. I had to. I needed inner peace and I was willing to do whatever it took to obtain it.

Well, after my first try at silence, I figured out the only way that I would be able to tolerate it would be if I was reading something. The next day, I was at Walmart again and I stopped in the book section to see if there was another book I could get to help me observe my moment of silence, without losing my mind.

This makes no sense but, I bought a book called *First Service* by Andrea Yeager. She was a tennis sensation I remembered hearing about when I lived in Dallas, TX. She had won about everything there was to win in the tennis world when she was just a teenager. This book was about what she had been doing after leaving tennis.

Apparently, she had dedicated her life and all of her earnings to help sick children. Once again, on the shelves of Walmart, I had found exactly what I needed. I loved children and I loved people who helped children so I bought the book and headed home to read myself into inner peace, or so I thought.

seven

i am not a big tennis fan, although I have played some, but even I could appreciate all of the hard work and dedication Andrea had gone through to achieve her extreme success. She was impressive. She was also irritating. She couldn't just tell her story of the great work she was doing after tennis with the sick kids and the ranch. No, she had to talk about God.

Here was a young athlete that had never once set foot in a church or read a Bible, and everything in the book was beginning to be about God. Really! God helped me do this and God showed me that and God, God, God, God, God! I was reading this book, in silence, so I could achieve some inner peace and be able to sleep at night. However, I was experiencing the exact opposite. This book with all of her talk about God was actually destroying what little peace I already had.

I was getting so angry every time she would talk about God that I thought I was going to explode. What made her think she was such an expert on God? Tennis player that had never been to church was suddenly an expert. Seriously, I was trying so hard to help myself that I read almost half of it. I wouldn't have made it through the second chapter if I hadn't been so determined to have silence every day.

Everybody has his or her breaking point and for me, it came about half way through the book. I was practically in a rage. I had to stop. The last thing I wanted to do was create any bad karma trying to achieve inner peace. I put the book down. I wasn't going to give up on the silence and inner peace but, I was done with *First Service*. I went to the bookshelf to look for something to read that didn't have anything about God in it so I could calm down and get back to business.

My husband keeps a nice collection of books he has read. I decided to look through them. The problem with that is almost all of Steve's books are huge, spy novels. There wasn't even one of them I was remotely interested in. I was serious about having some silence every day and I knew the only way I could tolerate it would be if I was reading something. At this point, I wanted something to read that didn't have any God stuff in it so much that I was willing to try anything. I lucked out at the last minute.

There, on the shelf, almost hidden by the huge spy novels was a little book Steve had bought years before when we were in Missouri. I think one of his sisters had told him about it. He came home with it, read about half a chapter and said he didn't like it. It was titled *Miracles of the Mind*. I picked it up and looked it over. It was perfect. It was about telepathic communication and scientific experiments dealing with it. Wouldn't have to worry about God being in this science book and so, I was back on the right track.

I read a little of *Miracles of the Mind* every day during my silent time. It was so boring it nearly put me to sleep but hey, at least I wasn't getting angry and irritated from reading it. I slowed down and didn't read as much at each setting. I was going to make this book last for three or four weeks, if I could.

The first half of the book was about the experiments the government conducted on telepathic communication. The second half was about the people involved with the experiments. Very unusual format, I thought but, I was reading every day and not getting upset so I just continued to read. I was nearing the end of the book when I started reading about a woman who had traveled to the Philippines to study and write about the Spiritual Healers people sought out from all over the world. They could supposedly cure anything from hemorrhoids to cancer with just their hands.

It was the first time since I started reading the book that I found it interesting. It was pretty amazing stuff although I didn't think I really believed any of it. The author was extremely skeptical in the beginning, too, but she was becoming a believer after all she was witnessing. It was near the end of her trip when she, herself, got sick.

She was in her hot little room and started suffering with something resembling a migraine headache. She was in excruciating pain and was so sick that she couldn't get out of bed to seek help. She laid there suffering for days. She started freaking out. She was scared she was going to die, in that hotel room, in a different country, away from her family. She didn't want to die and she didn't want to die like that, either. She was desperate. She wanted to go home. She didn't know what to do.

That's when she got the idea that she should pray. She wasn't religious at all and she didn't know how to pray but, she was desperate. Well, you will never guess what happened. She prayed. That's right. She cried out to God to come and help her and just like that, God came to her and healed her. Her pain left immediately but, it didn't just end there. Oh heavens no! He also told her He was going to help her to heal others!

I sat there in disbelief. How on earth could this have happened to me again? I felt like I had been hoodwinked. The rage inside started to grow. I threw the stupid book on the coffee table. I wanted to kill somebody. Are you kidding me? How the hell could I, a woman who avoided anything to do with God or religion, end up reading two books, back to back, and have them both end up being about women who had each encountered God? And even more, they had encountered God in their own lives, away from any church? I wanted to scream! A whole month wasted trying to get inner peace and ending up angrier than I could remember being in my life!

I started screaming. I didn't scream out loud. I didn't want to scare my little Katie. I started screaming in my head, in my thoughts. I screamed, "If there really is a God, why don't we all know Him? If there really is a God, where the hell is He? If there really is a God, why hasn't He ever helped me? If there really is a God, why doesn't everybody know Him and why doesn't He help everybody? If there really is a God, why don't I know you? If you're really real, then WHERE THE HELL ARE YOU?"

Immediately after I screamed that last question, to a God I didn't believe in, the strangest thing happened. I felt the presence of someone in the room with me and I heard the words *"I am here."*

I turned around to see who had come into my house to answer the questions that I had been screaming in my mind but, no one was there. But, someone was there. I knew it! I had literally just heard His voice. It was like no voice I had ever heard before. And I had felt His presence in the room with me. Sometimes you just know when someone is looking at you or when someone has entered a room. You feel it. It was like telepathic communication. Seriously! I was in shock. Had that just happened? Had God come into my house, into my living room and answered my question?

Tears streamed down my face. I was literally shaking. I remember letting out a little giggle. I was like the women in the two books that I had just been hating on. God was real. He really was. God heard me cry out and, He had answered me. I was sure of it. I had felt Him and heard His voice. God was real.

He really was. He had come to me, not in a church, but to me, where I was, to let me know He was real. I remember looking around with a goofy expression and from that moment on, I would never be the same again.

eight

i spent the rest of that Friday afternoon in a euphoric state, waiting for Steve to come home. Tears of joy streamed down my cheeks as smiles and giggles escaped from somewhere deep inside me. Almost immediately, fear also came. I would think from time to time, was I crazy? Was I losing my mind? Of course, I knew I wasn't but, that's what other people would think. What was I going to do? People were going to laugh at me and make fun of me when I told them what happened. Not telling anyone what had happened to me that day just wasn't an option. I had been transformed. Even if I didn't come out and tell people, they would know it because, I wasn't the same person anymore.

Panic had set in by the time Steve came home. The longer I waited to tell him, the worse it became. We were sitting on the patio watching the girls play in the backyard. I was trying to keep up with what he was telling me about his day. We had reached a pause in the conversation. I took a deep breath and told him something weird had happened to me. He asked what it was.

Trembling and teary-eyed, I told him that God had come to me in the living room when I was reading his book and that I had felt Him and heard Him and that I believe in God now. I glanced over to see the look on his face.

He was looking at me, and he just looked normal and said something like "Really?" Then, unplanned, I blurted out, "I think that lady I met the other day has been praying for me or something." Then, he said the strangest thing. "I have been praying for you every day."

Wait. What? He had been praying for me? When the heck did he do that and why didn't I know about it? That is when I said my own, "Really?"

During the afternoon hours of joy mixed with fear, I had also been feeling this strange urge as if I should go to the little Chapel inside the church. I told Steve I kind of wanted to go there after dinner, if he didn't mind. He said he didn't. We had dinner, I cleaned up and I went to the Chapel. I had never been there or even looked at it before. I just knew it was supposed to be open all of the time. And I knew I was supposed to go there, today.

Talk about feeling weird and being miles out of my comfort zone, I was a nervous wreck! I had no idea what I was supposed to do there.

I walked in and I think there were a couple of other people there. It was like a tiny church. There were two or three pews and many stained glass windows. It was pretty. I walked in and sat down and looked around, not knowing if I should kneel or what.

I didn't know how to pray so, I just said, "Thank you," silently, in my mind. Oh, how I wanted to hear His voice again! I waited for a long time but...nothing. I remember thinking, or maybe telling Him it was okay. He didn't have to talk to me again because He had spoken to me before, and once was enough. I thanked Him again and left.

nine

the next morning, I got up and went to the kitchen for a cup of coffee but, everything seemed different. It was a Saturday morning, like every other Saturday morning but I felt as if I didn't know what I was supposed to do. It's hard to explain. Maybe waking up with no memory feels like this to people who have had traumatic brain injuries. I remember smiling at Steve, a lot. I was sort of going through the motions. Who was I now and what was I supposed to be doing? I got the idea that I should keep reading.

I began to wonder what I should read next. There was a book referred to in the books I had just read. I went back and looked it up. It was titled *A Course in Miracles*. I knew there was a library in town and I asked Steve if I could run over and see if they had this book. I questioned the librarian about it when I got there and she knew of it. She told me it was checked out and also said that there was a sizable waiting list for it. I was disappointed but, told her I would try to find it somewhere else the next day. She insisted I put my name on the list anyway. I didn't see the point and I didn't want to waste my time doing it but, like I said, she insisted.

Sunday, we went to church and came home and had lunch and were just hanging at the house. I went to the grocery store to get something for dinner and when I got back, Steve told me the library had called and said they had the book I reserved. I couldn't believe it. How could it be? There were so many people's names ahead of mine on the list. I went over and sure enough, there it was. *A Course in Miracles* was on the shelf behind the checkout counter with my name on it. My first thought was that it was a miracle and God definitely wanted me to read it. My second thought was it was big. When I got home with it, I discovered it was like a college course book; there were three sections, the course, 365 days of lessons and a teacher's guide.

I am a high school dropout so to say it was a bit intimidating, would be an under-statement. I was determined to try so the next day I returned to my time of silence and reading in the afternoon. I started reading it but, I didn't understand anything I read. After a few days, I was convinced I was too dumb to read a book like that. I was ready to give up and take it back to the library so someone that deserved it could have it when, I decided to flip forward and look for something, anything that might make sense to me.

Then it happened. I was reading a page and suddenly, it was as if someone was speaking to me.

The words started to flow. It was the most beautiful way of talking I had ever heard. It started to make sense even though it was all new to me. When I started to read, a sense of peace would come over me that was like nothing I had ever experienced before. Then, I couldn't put it down. I found myself reading constantly, and every time I read, it was like being in Heaven. I was eating it up. I started marking pages I loved with rubber bands because I had so many pieces of paper in it to mark phrases and paragraphs I loved that, it was becoming quite the mess. How I wish I had taken a picture of the book after I got done with it! You wouldn't believe what it looked like.

Well, that week went by quickly. The next thing I knew, it was Saturday morning again, August 14. I was in the shower and the strangest thing happened. As I was washing my hair, with my eyes shut, I saw myself in a vision. I was in a different house and it was filled with foster kids. I saw myself gardening and playing baseball with them. It wasn't only me. Steve and the girls were there, too. It wasn't in Stillwater, though. It was back home in Missouri. It was so real and so weird. I hadn't thought that up. I wasn't even thinking about anything like that and I hadn't been. That's when I figured out it was a vision from God, and a mission. I hurried downstairs to tell Steve that God wanted us to go back home and become foster parents. We were supposed to have a lot more kids than we had before. I don't know what I expected him to say. I guess I must have assumed he would have jumped on board and gotten excited like me. It didn't happen. He said he hadn't had a vision like that, and that he wasn't going to do anything, until he did.

I think I might have caught a 'what the heck is wrong with you' look out of the corner of his eye, but then again, maybe not. I remember getting worried about how I was going to do what God wanted me to do if Steve wasn't going to help me. I was quiet the rest of the day, wondering who was going to help me and how I was going to do it. I knew I couldn't do it alone and be out there playing and gardening. I would be cooking, cleaning, and doing laundry all day, every day with that many kids.

The next morning, as I showered before church, I had the vision again. It was exactly the same, except for one thing. This time there was the shadow of an elderly woman in the kitchen with me. She was in the corner, folding laundry and humming. The kids were calling her Grandma as they came and went. That was it! God had shown me how I was going to do it. I was going to take in some elderly woman who needed a place to live and she was going to help me. I was so relieved. Only problem was how I was going to find a nice elderly woman who needed a place to live and wanted to help take care of a bunch of kids?

I thought about it all day. We went to the church picnic that night and I told the woman I thought had been praying for me, about what had happened to me. I also told her about the visions and that I would be going back to Missouri to do God's will. I didn't tell my husband about the second vision and how it was all going to work out fine, though. I got the feeling I should keep that to myself for a little while, so I did.

family photo album

My last Christmas at home with all of my children and my granddaughter.

Our Minnesota lake in January.

Steve and the girls working on the ice rink on the lake.

Courtney and Katie all decked out for the cold.

Me and the girls snowmobiling on the lake.

My little princesses Courtney and Katie.

Courtney with our new little Siamese kitten.

Joey fishing with Courtney after the thaw

Courtney and Katie ready to leave the lake and move to Stillwater

Katie, happy to finally be alone with mom.

The Adoration Chapel with the little tabernacle
on the right.

ten

i hadn't had insomnia since my conversion experience so I was a little distressed when it came back the following week. It was different this time. I would lay awake and see the visions of me, the foster kids, and a shadow of the old woman. On Saturday night, I had insomnia, again. It occurred to me that maybe it was God waking me up all along to get my attention. My sleeping hours were the only time I had ever had any silence before.

Maybe it was how he showed me I wasn't happy without him. As St. Augustine said, "Our hearts are restless until they rest in you." It made sense to me. So why was I awake now seeing these visions of me with all of the kids coming and going and the old woman folding laundry? Maybe God wanted to show me something about it. So, I asked, "What? What is it you want to show me that you can't show me when I'm awake?"

Immediately after I asked that question, the shadow went away and I saw the old woman. It was not good. It was the last person on the face of the earth that I would have wanted to see. It was my mother. Moreover, I instantly knew why it was her. God wanted me to forgive her. God wanted me to stop hating her. It was too much. It was asking more than what was possible. The tears came and then the sobs. How could He do this to me? I had just found out He was real and now He was telling me I couldn't be with Him as long as I hated her. I was heartbroken. I was becoming inconsolable so I climbed out of bed and went to the family room.

I always felt close to God when I was reading my Course so, I picked it up and tried to read through the tears. I was a mess. I started having a conversation with God in-between the pages and the sobs. I explained to Him that it was my mother's fault that I had hated Him all of those years. She was so mean and vile when she was drinking and she always brought up God stuff at the same time. One minute she'd be saying Jesus loved me and the next minute she would be cussing like a sailor. Any mention of anything religious always reminded me of her. It was why it made me sick to my stomach. I felt like He wanted me to tell Him all about it and all the terrible things that she had done, so I did.

I had lived with my mother for a little over seventeen years so there was a lot to tell. It took several hours, from midnight until five in the morning. I seemed to be able to remember every mean, hateful thing she had ever done or said to me and I told him all about it. (It was in my mind, like telepathic communication). Finally, I was done. I was numb by this time. I sat there with my book on my lap, exhausted and numb.

After a while, God asked me a question. He asked me if I would be willing to let Him show me what He sees, when He looks at my mother. I sat there spent, considering His request for some time. I didn't really see what it would hurt so I said, "Sure." Then, it was as if He was showing me how He felt when He saw all of the things she had done. It made Him sad and He was disappointed but, He still loved her and He still watched and waited, hoping she would do better. What I saw was someone, a lot like me, who tried to do the right thing but had messed up a lot. I saw someone who had been through some bad things and I saw someone who made many mistakes. I saw my mother, not through the eyes of a hurt child. I saw my mother through the Eyes of Mercy.

It is impossible to describe what I experienced that morning. The hatred and resentment and hurt I carried around with me all of those many years, were somehow lifted off of me. I cannot say that I forgave her. It wasn't me. What I had done was give it to Him. And it was gone. He had taken it away. At the very instant I agreed to let Him show me what He saw when He looked at her, I felt as if I was filled with love, with grace, as if the flood gates were opened and I was being showered. I have never, in my life, experienced anything like it. I knew forgiveness was simultaneous. I knew the little word "as" in the bible in the phrase *...forgive us our trespasses as we forgive those who trespass against us,* was the biggest, most important word in the bible. I couldn't believe that I didn't hate my mother anymore but, I didn't. Then I realized I could still be with the God I had just met. Gratefulness filled my being and the tears flowed. I just thanked Him over and over.

Then my husband walked into the room, looked at me, puzzled, and asked me what was wrong. I told him I had been up all night, fighting with God. I told Him God had told me I had to forgive my mother and I had told Him I couldn't and after going around and around with Him all night, I had finally been able to do it. I smiled and told Steve I didn't hate her anymore. Steve knew as well as anyone about my mother. He realized something had happened that night but he had a worried look on his face.

eleven

i was basking in joy for several days after my all-nighter with God. I also couldn't put down *A Course in Miracles*. We were getting ready for a trip to Missouri before school started and I realized that I was going to have to tell the boys about what had happened to me. I told Steve I needed to be a mirror and reflect God's love to the people I met. He looked thrilled. I finished the book on the way to Missouri.

I decided to try telling my conversion story out on his friends in Kansas City that we stopped to see on the way back home. You know, people really want to talk about baseball and concerts and funny things they have heard. Nobody really wants to hear about how you didn't believe in God, and then a series of miraculous things happened and now you believe. I really felt as if I was supposed to share what happened to me, though, so I did. I was uncomfortable, they were uncomfortable and Steve was really uncomfortable, but I got through it. I'm pretty sure they were glad to see us leave, me anyway.

For me, talking about God with anyone was like trying to speak a new language in a foreign country. I knew something significant had happened to me but I wasn't sure how to go about expressing it. I am glad I had my first attempt with the people in KC, it made it a little easier when I told my boys. I gathered them around at my oldest son's house and I said I had something to tell them. They looked like they were expecting me to tell them I had cancer or something. They didn't know what to say after I finished telling them I believed in God now and I had forgiven my mother. It was okay, though. They didn't laugh at me and call me a Jesus freak or anything. I did get the feeling that they believed me and knew I wasn't just going crazy.

I had the thought I should tell my mother what had happened. When I thought about it more, I couldn't really tell her how I had forgiven her and didn't hate her anymore without telling her that I did hate her. I don't really think she ever knew it. I think she always thought we were angry with her from time to time and that was it. Telling her I had forgiven her would only hurt her. Besides, I hadn't really done it, God had.

I was beginning to understand that somehow, this forgiveness thing wasn't as much about other people and me as it was about God and me. It was a personal thing only we could understand. When I got home, I sent her an email and apologized for not keeping in touch, as I should and that I would love to hear from her. That's all it took. I would learn rather quickly even though the hate, resentment, and hurt were gone, I could still get irritated and that was kind of a bummer. I guess I had thought everything would be happy, beautiful, and heavenly now that I had God and the Holy Spirit. It was not what God had planned, however. It was fall. It was back to school time and He was ready to teach me a thing or two.

twelve

School started. Courtney was in first grade. Katie started kindergarten. Steve started a class for a couple of hours in the evenings called Catechism. We went to church that next Sunday and when I was walking in, I had a weird thought. If I had God and the Holy Spirit, and if I had had a conversion experience in my own house, why did I need Jesus and why did I need to go to church? I asked Steve and he told me I needed them both. We went to the Wild Rice Festival and I saw my new friend and asked her the same thing. She said the same thing Steve said. I couldn't understand it. I ran into a young priest at school the next week and asked him the same thing and he said, "Oh, you need them." What they didn't tell me was why I needed them.

Back to school was a busy time for the school and the church. Steve loved his class and he was always talking about it and the guy who was teaching it. I guess he had started a group called the Catholic Workers and they had bought houses, refurbished them, and opened them up for homeless women and children. I had worked with a couple of moms and their babies in foster care in Missouri so I was interested to learn more about it

The next Sunday, they had God's Right Hand Fair after church. All of the different church groups had displays in the social hall with information about them and sign-up sheets if you wanted to volunteer. Steve went straight to the Catholic Worker display and signed up. I was drawn to a display about the little Chapel I had gone to the first night I believed.

It was called an Adoration Chapel and people signed up for each hour of the day, seven days a week. That way, someone was always there praying. They had a sign-up sheet for open spots. One spot was listed as "urgent need." It was on Wednesdays from 4-5 in the morning. I signed up. No one called either one of us by Tuesday afternoon, so I called and told them I had signed up for the urgent hour. I told them that I wasn't a Catholic and asked them if I could do it and they said it was fine.

I started the next morning. I set the clock but I didn't really need to because I was so worried I would miss it, I never really slept on Tuesday nights. I did the hour for almost two years. I saw the lady that went before me was there from 2-4. I started going in early incase she was tired and wanted to leave. Occasionally she would but most mornings, she stayed until four or even later.

I started reading *A Course in Miracles* again. It was as if I had never read it before. It was all new and more beautiful than I remembered. It is what I did in the chapel during my hour. I filled myself with the soul changing words of peace I read in that book. I started writing down my favorite phrases and paragraphs. I probably have copied that book word for word a couple of times, at least.

My new friend had given me a book about Fatima. She was always telling me how great our church and faith were. Steve read the book and started immediately praying a Rosary every morning. He asked me to do it with him one Saturday and I did. He gave me a pamphlet with the words and a rosary. I did it with him. I hated it. It was just saying these words repeatedly and I couldn't see the point. I couldn't understand why he would choose to do that when he could talk to God instead. I started telling him how God told me this and God told me that.

He started to ask questions like, "What do you mean? Are you hearing voices? That isn't normal. Don't you think you should talk to someone?" He thought it was fine if all of a sudden, he wanted to start praying this rosary thing but he thought it was somewhat weird I was talking to God all the time. He would say, "God doesn't want to know about every single little decision you need to make."

I would say, "Yes, He does."

Every time I went anywhere, I drove by the Catholic Worker House he was always talking about. I knew everything that had to do with the house was done by volunteers. I drove by for two or three weeks and the weeds all around the house kept getting taller and taller. It looked terrible. One

Saturday, on the way home from the store, I couldn't stand it anymore.

I pulled into the driveway and knocked on the door. A woman answered and I told her my name and asked her if she minded if I mowed the grass. She said it was okay so I went home, put the groceries away and went upstairs where Steve was watching college football. I told him I was going to mow the Catholic Worker House's yard.

He came along to help me. We had just started mowing when a white van pulled into the driveway. I was so scared it was someone who was coming to mow and I had messed up his or her plans. That wasn't the case at all. It was the man who taught Steve's class. He was the guy who had started the houses and he saw us mowing and stopped to say. "Thank you." Boy, was I relieved.

He took us on a tour of the house and I met one of the women who lived there and her children. He invited me to join the Ladies Catechism Class he also taught and told us about their Friday night gatherings. We started going. He was so nice. Our lives were changing so much I barely recognized us. My favorite phrases were becoming, "I can't believe I believe!" and "Who are we?"

For some reason, my favorite part of each week was the hour I would spend in the Adoration Chapel. I thought about it all week. I looked forward to it all week. I would be exhausted during the day but then, I couldn't wait to do it again. I don't know why it brought me so much peace but, it did. Then, one morning, while I was reading in the Chapel, I had a realization. The person that was talking to me through the words of that book was Jesus! What? I went back to the beginning and reread the preface. This book was from Jesus Christ.

That is why it said things like *my* cross and *I am the Atonement*. I read the words: I have been correctly referred to as *the Lamb of God*. I felt so stupid. Jesus is the one who came into my room and said, *I am here*. Jesus is the one who listened to me all night and helped me forgive my mother. Jesus is the reason for everything and I had been walking around saying, "Who needs Jesus?" and being happy I wasn't a *Jesus freak*. I felt like such a fool. I was happy that I knew it, finally but, I was embarrassed.

It did make sense, though. I remembered hearing the words … *no one can come to the Father except through me.* If Jesus was the one we would meet after we died to judge us, the fact I had gotten a direct line to God without Him just proved what a fool I was. Jesus was the way, the truth and the life. He was Mercy itself. He had shown me my mother the way He saw her. Was it humbling or humiliating? A bit of both, I think. There would be many more moments like that in the future.

thirteen

September 11 fell on a Saturday. I had gone to the basement to do my ironing for the upcoming week. I turned on the TV and every station was reliving the terrorist attacks. I kept flipping the channels because I didn't want to see it again. I happened upon a nun, sitting in a chair, talking. I started ironing and listening to her. She was quite amusing. She was talking about lying. I ended up watching the entire episode. As I finished my ironing, I remember thinking how glad I was that I wasn't a liar and went to bed.

The next day, September 12, we went to church. The readings were about the prodigal son. The young priest gave the homily for the day. It was interesting. My dad always called himself the prodigal son of his family and I knew the story from my childhood. But, he told us many things about the story I had never heard before. He told us about the gifts the father had given the son. The first one was a robe and he explained what it meant. Then he gave him a ring and he explained what that meant. Lastly, he gave him sandals. He explained the symbolism behind the sandals was that the son, was free to go again, if he so chose. The father didn't want him to ever leave again but he wasn't going to take away his freedom to do so. I was beginning to realize that the more I knew, the more I knew how much I didn't know. Every story in the Bible is like that. Layers and layers of meanings and symbolisms.

That night, insomnia came again. I was smart this time. Right away, I asked what it was I needed to learn. I was not expecting the answer I got. He said, *"My child, you cannot be a liar, anymore."* The night before, I had been happy I wasn't a liar and now, Jesus was calling me a liar. Wow. Wrong again! I knew instantly what He was talking about, though. And I realized I was a liar.

I had decided, right after we adopted Courtney, I was never going to tell her she was adopted. I said I didn't want her to ever think that she wasn't wanted or loved. I had started lying to her almost immediately. She would ask where her baby pictures were and I would say we didn't have a camera when she was a little baby. She would ask me why her eyes were brown and everybody else had blue eyes, and I would make up something else. I was a liar. I really was. Then He showed me my real reason for lying to her. I didn't want to give her sandals. I had watched my own mother spend years and years trying to find her biological mother. I was afraid that Courtney would do the same thing one day and then leave me. I was worse than a liar. I was a selfish liar.

How Jesus was teaching me was unbelievable. The nun on TV wasn't an accident. The homily that morning wasn't an accident. He was orchestrating everything. He had been orchestrating everything all along. How did He do this stuff? I knew, especially after what had happened when He told me I had to stop hating my mother, I had to stop lying. The next morning, I told Steve God had told me I had to tell Courtney the truth. He thought it was a bad idea. But I insisted I couldn't lie to her anymore. I know he was getting sick of me saying God told me stuff but he just asked me to think about it a little more and wait.

I worried all day about what I was going to do. I couldn't lie anymore but, I didn't want to make my husband mad. That afternoon, I had a weird thought. Maybe I should talk to someone about this. I got the church bulletin, looked up the priest's phone number and called it. He answered. I told him I had a problem and needed some advice.

He said to come on up. I couldn't believe he answered and had time for me. I ran right up there and told him my story. He was so wonderful. He said I had to stop lying, that was for sure, he chuckled but, he said that I needed to wait until my husband was ready and we needed to tell her together. He was very adamant on that. I thanked him and left. I had time before the girls got out of school so I ran over to the Adoration Chapel. I was kneeling when I went there by this time. I knelt down and asked simply, "How am I going to tell her?" Then, miraculously, I heard my own voice (in my head) and I was telling a story.

Once upon a time, there was a man and his wife who were very much in love. More than anything, they wanted a baby of their own. One day, they found out they were having a baby girl. They decided to name her Hannah Leigh. They were both so happy. Then, something went wrong. The baby girl they had been dreaming about was stillborn. It means she was born dead.

They were broken hearted and so, so sad. God decided He wanted to give them a gift to make them happy again. And so, he gave them a different little girl and her name was Courtney. Then they were all happy. I couldn't believe it. He had answered me better than I could have ever imagined. Then, I realized that it was September 13. It was Hannah's birth/death day. I knew at that moment, it was the day I was supposed to tell my beautiful baby girl the truth and Jesus had just given me the words to say.

When Steve got home, I told him about going to see the priest and about the Adoration Chapel. I reminded him what day it was. He agreed to tell her the truth so, after dinner and baths. We took the girls into our room, and we all got on the bed and I told them the story I had heard in the Chapel that day, word for word. I wish you could have seen little Courtney. She was beaming. She sat up, clapped her hands, and said, "I knew it! I knew it!" She had the biggest smile on her face and then she said, "Tell it again Mommy!" So, I did.

fourteen

that lesson learned, now onto the next. Jesus wasn't wasting any time. I have to go back in time for this chapter. When Steve and I were going through the marriage prep with the priest in Missouri, I had agreed to let our future children go to a Catholic School. Steve had started telling me how much better it would be if our household/family were all the same religion. It made sense. He said I wouldn't like it if our children could go to Communion with him but I couldn't. He kept on and on about how it would be better for everyone if we were all on the same page. So, I agreed to join RCIA and become Catholic for the good of our family. I also signed Joey up for classes so he could be Catholic, too. Joey loved the classes so much. I had never seen him so comfortable and enjoying a class like that.

I, of course (it was extremely uncomfortable because I didn't believe in God anymore, you know) wasn't having as much fun as Joey but, I was all about family and being together, so I persevered.

I was missing ER, a new TV show that was on every Thursday night, to go to this class to become Catholic. It was a real sacrifice on my part. Everything was going okay until we got to the place in the class where they were explaining what Catholics believed about the Eucharist. At that point, we had a problem. They told me that night Catholics believed that when the priest consecrated the bread and wine, it truly became the body and blood of Jesus Christ.

Excuse me? Are you kidding me? You mean to tell me you really believe bread and wine somehow become flesh and blood? I just sat there with my mouth shut and thought, "You people are crazy!"

I went home and told Steve we had a problem. I told him they said they really believed the bread and wine became flesh and blood. I had been a Baptist as a child and I knew when those words were spoken, it was symbolic. I said, "Can you believe that is what they really believe?" I wasn't even ready for his response. He told me that is what he really believed. He told me every Sunday, when we went to church, and the priest said the words of Consecration, he really believed a miracle happened upon the altar and the bread and wine really did become the body and blood of Christ.

I had one of my best poker face moments I think I have ever had in my life. I just looked at him calmly and in my mind, I started screaming at the top of my lungs... "Oh my God! What have I done? I've sold my home and moved my boys in with an f-ing LUNATIC! What is he telling me? Nobody in his right mind can believe this!"

I was in a state of panic. What had I done to my boys and myself? How could I be with a crazy man? But, I loved him. I started weighing my options. He loved me. He treated me like a queen. He wanted to marry me and he was a decent man. He treated my boys with respect and wanted to be a good influence in their lives. They liked him. He didn't look crazy. This was the only crazy thing there was about him.

I had been married to an abusive, mean, alcoholic jerk and now I was with a really wonderful guy who believed this one really stupid thing. I made the decision at that moment to ignore this stupid religious thing and be thankful for the wonderful man who had come into my life. I didn't want to ever discuss it again, but, I did have to tell him there was no way in hell I was ever going to say I believed it.

I told him. He said I didn't have to believe it all; I just needed to keep my mind open to the possibility. I told him I may not be the best person in the world but, I was sure as hell not a hypocrite and I would never, ever say I believed something that I didn't believe. I had scruples and I dropped out of class. I also took Joey out of his class because, he was my boy and if I couldn't be Catholic, he couldn't either.

Steve was disappointed, I think, but he never made me feel bad about my decision. That's the kind of man he is.

Now, back to the present. I had stopped lying to my baby girl. I was still going to the Chapel and I was still rereading *A Course in Miracles*. Jesus was real. He was in my life. He was transforming me.

And, then, as I was reading my book, in the Chapel, He explained to me what He really meant when He said those words. We don't need flesh and blood to sustain us. We get plenty of that. He didn't suffer and die to save our bodies. It was our souls He came to save. He wanted us in Heaven with Him and God.

What we really need is food for our souls. That is what Jesus is giving us. He is giving us his spiritual body and his spiritual blood to feed our spirits. We needed nourishment for our souls. It made sense. Our souls are what Jesus really cares about. I got it! So I called Steve, at work, and told him I got it. I understood the Eucharist. I was so excited to tell him I could finally say I believed what he believed. He wasn't sure I really understood it correctly but, he was happy that I finally wanted to become Catholic.

fifteen

right after I had the revelation about the Eucharist, I had another all night insomnia episode. I understood Jesus wasn't giving me these graces and gifts just for me. He had work for me to do. I was supposed to share what I had received. He wanted me to help other people know Him and, He wanted me to write a book.

I was ready to try to help other people know Him but, I was a high school dropout and I didn't know the first thing about writing a book. In addition, me sharing my story, wasn't really having the effect on people of them wanting to convert. My husband was looking at me as if I was crazy and the people in Kansas City had been very polite but, I got the feeling they thought I was crazy, too.

They certainly hadn't asked me any questions or tried to get me to talk about it more or explain anything. Then, He made me understand this wasn't something I could do on my own. It was like the Apostles trying to preach after the Ascension. They were ineffective. Then they received the Holy Spirit in the Upper Room and were able to baptize 3000 the next day.

I needed Him to help me. I needed His strength. All of a sudden, I was consumed with desire to have the Eucharist. I felt as if I were going to die without it. Someone this dumb, stupid, and wrong all the time wouldn't be able to do anything without His help. I wanted the Eucharist more than anything. I needed it. I couldn't stop until I had it.

As the wee hours of the morning passed, I read my book and started thinking about how I could write a book to help people, like me, find Jesus. Then, I felt like He was telling me the guy that taught Steve's class was supposed to help me. I made an outline and then I woke Steve up thirty minutes early so I could tell him what had happened during the night.

I had volunteered to help with picture day at the girls' school in a couple of hours. Steve suggested I try to talk to the priest again. It sounded like a good plan to me so I got the girls up and ready for school and off we went.

I saw the young priest I had asked, "Who needs Jesus and why do we need the church?" I asked if I could talk to him a minute. He said he was too busy. Go figure!

Then I saw the older priest I had talked to about my lying and he said he had meetings all morning. I was tired. I was disappointed. But, I had volunteered to help out so, I spent the morning helping get forms with kids and I also saw a lot of cute smiles as they took everyone's picture.

When I was done helping, I walked through the cafeteria on my way out and I saw a deacon. He was a good friend of the lady that had given me the book on Fatima. I asked if I could talk to him a minute, he agreed. I told him about how I was supposed to write a book and who was going to help me. He chuckled like I was crazy.

"Oh really!" he said.

Then I told him I felt like I was going to die if I didn't receive the Eucharist. We talked off and on throughout the day and at the end of the day he told me that if I wanted to receive the Eucharist as badly as I said I did, then I needed to join RCIA and become Catholic and do it the right way. I told Steve and he agreed. I called the next morning and signed up. Can you believe it?

The girl who had walked away from RCIA in Missouri, could hardly wait to start in Minnesota. It was unbelievable. Steve really wanted me to go to the classes on the Catechism he was enjoying so much so, I signed up for them, too. Besides, the teacher was supposed to help me write my book, right. I was determined to become Catholic. Who would have ever believed it? Certainly not me.

sixteen

there was one thing the Catechism and RCIA classes I had signed up for had in common. It was a cute little 78-year-old woman. Don't ask me why but, she and I would very quickly become best of friends. More than anything, I was a student who wanted to learn everything I could about the Catholic faith and she was a single woman who had spent years teaching religion to children at a Catholic school in Kansas. We hit it off immediately. We would go to the Catechism class on Tuesday nights and then we would sit together at the RCIA class on Thursday nights.

We decided to meet on Thursday afternoons at Joseph's Restaurant and over pie and coffee, she would answer all of the questions I had from the previous week. In addition, we would talk on the phone from time to time. She would tell me later she had been in the Adoration Chapel praying one day and she had asked God to give her one close friend and then she had met me. It didn't take too long to find out why she didn't have many close friends.

To hear my new friend talk, you would think that she really disliked most of the people she met and she could hang onto a grudge forever. A lot of time was spent with her telling me who did this and who did that to hurt her or make her angry every time we got together. The next time we met, she would repeat the same things. She used to pray Novenas for intentions like getting the opportunity to tell off the doctor who made her mad and things like that. She was a deal, for sure. Eventually, as we got to know each other better, I could laugh at her and say I didn't think God was going to answer a prayer for revenge and she would laugh, too and say, "Maybe, not." But that didn't stop her. She was persistent.

My new "mentor" was Catholic since birth, and knew everything there was to know about it. Sometimes it seemed as if she really didn't get it or wasn't able to translate it into living. I, on the other hand, was having a relationship with Jesus and He was teaching me how to apply His teachings in my day-to-day life. She would be amazed when I told her some of the things that were going on with me and at the end of the day, she not only taught me but I taught her, as well. We were perfect together. She got mad at me from time to time, of course, but she never stayed mad at me. I think one of the biggest lessons she learned from me was that we could disagree once in a while and still be friends. It really didn't have to be: my way or the highway.

It was getting close to Christmas and our

discussion in RCIA turned to Purgatory. This is a hard lesson to understand for people raised in other religions because, Catholics are the only ones who believe in Purgatory, I think. Most Christians say after you die, you go either to Heaven or Hell, but Catholics believe you can need purification and in that case, you go to Purgatory until you are ready for Heaven.

A big discussion ensued and my friend kept insisting there most definitely was a Purgatory and another person in the class, that should have known better, kept saying that he didn't believe God would forgive us and then tell us we still have to pay for what we had done wrong. "You better believe you're going to have to pay!" my friend would say. Well, time ran out, thankfully, before the class ended up in a big argument but not before the girl I had met at the Catholic Worker House said she didn't think what my friend was saying made any sense. Well, she might as well have said, "You are stupid and don't know what you're talking about!" because that is how my friend took it. I would hear about it every time we talked for the next three or four years!

seventeen

Jesus instructed the Holy Spirit to teach me about Purgatory the next day. On Fridays, I would clean bathrooms and dust and mop to get the house ready for the weekend. I wanted to spend the majority of my time with Steve and the girls while we were all together.

As I was getting ready to start cleaning, I had the strongest urge to start writing my Christmas cards. It was earlier than I normally did them but, I couldn't shake the feeling I needed to get them done. I fixed a cup of coffee and got a box of cards and then I remembered the prayer I had prayed that morning. It was called the Prayer of Jabez.

With this prayer, you ask God to bless you as much as He wants, not as much as you want him to. You ask Him to increase your territory. In other words, the amount of people you witness to and you ask God to keep you from the evil one so you don't cause any more pain. As I opened up the address book, I realized my Christmas cards this year were going to be an opportunity to witness about what Jesus was doing in our lives. I could write about my conversion and the classes we were taking. I could explain I was going to become Catholic at the Easter Vigil. These cards were going to be different from any I had ever sent, or received before. I smiled, in spite of the butterflies in my stomach.

I opened the address book and looked for the first name. It was in the B's. It was the name of friends of Steve's from where he used to work before we got married. I had met them once and I knew they were Catholic and would probably be happy to hear my news, rather than think I was crazy for sharing it. I wrote a nice note in their card and looked at their address. They lived on Glover's Ford Road.

As I looked at the address, I remembered someone else I knew who lived on the same road. I babysat for her little boy for a little over a year. He was Katie's age and the two of them had been best little friends. He was the only little boy I had for a long time. He had a brother who was in grade school, so it seemed like he got sick a lot. He had hand, foot and mouth disease in the spring or early summer and then he had it again right after Halloween.

This disease makes the babies feel terrible. All they do is cry and want to be held for two or three days. It's contagious, too and they run a fever. When he started getting sick, I figured out right away what it was and I called his mom at work to come and get him. She never liked leaving work but it was necessary. She was mad when she got to my house and made some comments about how she didn't like him being around all of those *foster kids* and getting sick all the time.

Let me tell you. I have always had a *no tolerance policy* with people who make me mad or want to bad-mouth my kids and my foster kids were like my kids.

He wasn't getting sick from us. No one else had it the first time or this time. It was only him. The more I thought about it, the madder I got. I called her that evening and told her not to bring him back.

I finished the first envelope and did a couple more cards. I couldn't quit thinking about her. I knew she had probably been mad and didn't really mean what she said. I also knew she probably had a terrible weekend trying to find a new sitter to watch her sick little boy. I knew what I had to do. I got out a card and I wrote about how I had become a Christian and how Jesus had changed me, and I offered her the most heartfelt, sincere apology I could write with tears streaming down my face and I asked her to forgive me.

As the tears flowed, so did the grace. I wish I could tell you she was the only one I needed to apologize to but, she wasn't. There was my twin sister I hadn't spoken to in over fifteen years. There was one of Steve's sisters. There was the lady across the street from me that quit talking to me one day and instead of asking her what was wrong, I just quit talking to her, too.

One of the hardest cards I had to write that year was to a good friend of former boss. I had found a leather jacket that had been left at the bar one night and after a couple of days with no one coming back for it, I took it home and gave it to my husband. The next week, the guy who left it came in to get it. He was my boss's good friend and I was mortified. I said nothing. I could tell he was mad and I'm sure my boss was, also. I had been too scared to tell the truth and embarrass myself or my boss. I actually had to get a piece of notebook paper to write this one on and put it inside of the Christmas card. I told him what I had done and that I didn't realize it was his jacket. I told him how much of a coward I was back then.

I told him about my conversion and that I had to tell him the truth. I wrote the most sincere apology that I could. I asked him to forgive me and I also put $200.00 in the envelope. The hardest thing about this was having to sign my name. I was tempted to send it anonymously but, I knew that wouldn't be right. I also knew if I signed my name, he might tell my boss. I was so worried he would never forgive me. But, hard as it was, in the end, I did the right thing. I signed my name and put it in the mail with the others.

Even though I had cried my way through my Christmas card list that year, I had a sense of peace. I believe the Holy Spirit had shown me what it meant to pay for the wrongs we have committed. If you rob a bank and then become a Christian, you have to give the money back. If you hurt someone and then become a Christian, you have to apologize. If you have wronged someone and then become a Christian, you have to try to make it right

It isn't enough that Jesus forgives us and loves us. It is impossible understand fully all of the consequences of our actions. When we are rude to someone they can take it out on someone else. It goes on and on. We don't see the big picture until after we leave this earth. All I know is that if we are able to do anything to right our wrongs, we need to do it.

I believe nothing shows our Lord's mercy as much as Purgatory. I'm sure after I see the big picture and realize how many people have been hurt by my words and actions. I will know just exactly how much I owe. I wouldn't stand a chance of ever getting into Heaven without it. I felt I had started my purification right here on earth after I finished my Christmas cards that year.

Some of the people who I sent my apologetic Christmas cards to that year responded immediately. Some, I never heard from. Their responses weren't what was important for me. Writing them is what I needed to do. I had a sense, again, it was more between Jesus and me than between them and me. I did stop by my boss's house that next summer when I was home, to let him see my girls. He brought up the card. My heart dropped. He told me that his friend was so touched by it that he had brought it over to the bar and read it to my boss and everybody who was around. They weren't mad at me. They didn't hate me. They respected me and loved me for having the courage to do the right thing after all those years. He said they all thought I was an inspiration. I still cry, even as I write this, thinking about it.

Mercy is everywhere. My boss died a few years ago. I remember the preacher talking at his funeral and saying he had called him to come over to the hospital before he died. He said he had a hard time but had tried to make a confession and ask forgiveness. It made my heart so happy when I heard it. I don't know if my letter had anything to do with him doing that or not but, I have always hoped that it did.

eighteen

As you now know from my apologetic Christmas cards, I have done many wrong and bad things in my life. There are two things I did when I was a teenager that have actually haunted me my whole life. These two incidents are what would keep me awake at night. Of all of the bad things that I had done over forty-some years, these two infractions were the ones I had never been able to forget or put out of my mind.

They seem like minor things compared to some of the bigger sins that could have been burned into my conscience but, for some reason, it has always been just these two.

The first was when I was sixteen years old. I was living in Dallas, Texas and working at a steakhouse after school. It was the early seventies. A family came in for dinner one night with their son, in a wheelchair. He was clearly an injured Vietnam War vet. I don't want to make excuses for myself but, I don't really know why I did what I did. I looked at the guy in the wheelchair like I hated him. I wanted him to know I thought he was despicable, like someone who had intentionally murdered innocent women and children. The way I looked at him was venomous. I wanted to hurt him, even though I didn't even know him. I believe I accomplished that.

The second thing I did was after I had run away from home, when I was seventeen. I was living in an upstairs apartment with my boyfriend. We both happened to be in the kitchen one afternoon when kids were walking home from the neighborhood schools. I saw a boy walking all alone under the water tower near our house. I went over to the window and yelled, "Hey, Fatso!" at him. It is hard to explain how this happened but, at the instant I yelled at him, he turned and looked at me, and our eyes met. I was immediately mortified at what I had done. So was my boyfriend. He couldn't believe what I had done. Frankly, I couldn't either. I will always remember the hurt in that kid's eyes.

When I told my husband the two awful things I had done when I was a kid, he laughed and said all kids did stupid stuff like that once or twice in their lives.

Maybe they have and maybe they haven't. All I know is these two things had been with me, ever since they happened, year after year. As we were preparing for our first reconciliations in RCIA, my insomnia came back along with the two terrible things I had done in my youth.

We were learning about penance and I realized there was never going to be a way for me to find out who these two boys were. I would never be able to apologize or make up for what I had done. But, then again, there were many people I would never know, or be able to find, who I owed apologies to. So, I knew it had to be more than that. I couldn't figure out why those two guys haunted me instead of the hundreds of others. As I lay awake one night, reliving the pain I had caused each of them, I asked Jesus to tell me why it was I was continually haunted by these two things. What made them different?

After a while, I heard Him say, *"Those two times were the times I personally came down from Heaven to see you, and that is how you treated me."*

Believe me when I tell you those words are not something you ever, ever want to hear from Our Lord. I felt as if I had the wind knocked out of me. I couldn't believe it. I didn't want to. At the same time, it finally made sense. It explained everything.

I learned that night, what true contrition was. I cried my eyes out all night as I begged Him, over and over, to forgive me, and to give me another chance.

nineteen

RCIA and the Catechism classes consumed me, not to mention all that was going on with me, personally, in the wee hours. It was February and I needed to focus some attention on my family. My oldest son was expecting my first grandson around Valentine's Day. We knew it was going to be via scheduled C-section. I was trying to decide if I should go for the birth or go a day or two after when she would be coming home with the baby and I might be able to help them out by cooking and babysitting. I was torn. I wanted to be there for both! It was a ten-hour drive and the problem was my girls were in school now. I couldn't take off for a week, anyway, I didn't think I should, although I really wanted to.

As I toyed with what to do, my husband decided to make matters worse. He started insisting he didn't want me to take the girls with me this time. I had always taken them with me everywhere. I couldn't imagine being that far away from them!

What if they needed me? I would be ten hours away!

I was as adamant about taking them, as he was about me not taking them. I had refused to go on an all-expense paid, weeklong vacation to Mexico with him once when they were babies because I wouldn't have been able to enjoy myself being a whole country away!

He won the trip at work and was so upset with me but, in the end, he took his good friend and the two of them had a blast. This wasn't about getting even or anything. He kept saying he was afraid I was going to have a wreck and he didn't want to lose all of us.

I know I may have been partly responsible for his fears. I had made the trip with the girls once before and had found myself too tired to drive when I got to the Missouri border. I had stopped and gotten a room. My cell phone was out of range however, so I couldn't tell anyone until the next morning. We went round and round for days. He wasn't letting up at all. He wanted them home, in school, where they were supposed to be. I finally gave in. I told my son I would come and stay for three days when they brought the baby home.

I decided to put the girls to bed before I left, and drive through the night so I could minimize the time away from them. I had written a page long poem and put together a scavenger hunt so in the mornings, they could read the clues and go find a surprise that I had hidden for them, and then, the same thing for the evening. I had new books and coloring books and toys hidden all over the house.

You probably think I'm nuts but, it was the first time I had ever been away from my little Katie overnight. She was very attached to me and I wanted to do anything I could to make it easier for her.

They fell asleep and I got up, kissed my stubborn husband good-bye and headed out. I stopped in Albert Lea and filled up the car with gas. My plan was to try to drive straight through Iowa without stopping so I wouldn't have to freeze to death gassing up. I set the cruise control to the highest speed I could without drawing too much attention to myself. I scoured the landscape, looking for highway patrol and I flew through Iowa State without stopping once. Thank goodness for that because it was really windy and really cold.

When I crossed into Missouri, the sun was just beginning to come up. I had to make the first truck stop, which was in Bethany, as I was almost out of gas, literally me and the car. I filled up and got coffee.

I breathed in the cold, brisk air to help wake me up. I knew my little girls would be waking up soon, without me and that made me sad. It was still freezing but, everything in Missouri always seemed to be better and it was feeling good to be home.

I started the car, refreshed and feeling excited to see my family, and eased up to the highway. I had to cross the overpass and make a left to get back onto Highway 35 south to Kansas City. As I waited for a couple of trucks to go by, I saw something on the overpass. It looked like a man walking on the side of the highway with a duffle rolled up on his shoulder. "What is this?" I thought. And then, that familiar voice I heard from time to time said, *"This is your chance."*

I was immediately overcome with fear. This couldn't be the chance that I had begged for. No! It couldn't be this. This was crazy. This was dangerous. Jesus would never expect me to risk my life for another chance, would He?

I started screaming at the top of my lungs, in my mind. "No! This isn't my chance! I can't do this!"

Again, I heard, *"This is your chance."*

I started arguing with Him telling Him I couldn't do this. I would be a terrible mother and wife if I put my life at risk like this. What would happen to my husband and girls if I was killed by a hitchhiker?

Then He said, *"Don't you trust me? There are no coincidences."*

When He said that, I immediately understood my husband's unreasonable insistence that I not bring the girls. Of course, it wouldn't be an option to pick up a hitchhiker with my girls in the car. That is why I was alone. "But I'm scared! I can't do it!"

He answered, *"This is your chance. Trust me. There are no coincidences."*

My eyes were fixed on the hitchhiker as I pulled out on the highway. The thoughts in my head were keeping time with my heart pounding out of my chest. WHAT DO I DO? WHAT DO I DO? WHAT DO I DO? WHAT DO I DO? I was overcome with the fear of letting a strange man in my car. I was even more afraid of leaving Jesus standing on the side of the road, in the cold. WHAT DO I DO? WHAT DO I DO? WHAT DO I DO? WHAT DO I DO? I was in a state of panic.

And again I heard, *"This is your chance. Trust me. There are no coincidences."*

I have never been so scared in my life. Well, speaking of coincidences, as I crossed the overpass, he had reached the on-ramp. He was actually crossing the road directly in front of me. I had to slow down or hit him. *"There are no coincidences."*

I was practically hyperventilating when I rolled down the window and asked, "Where are you going?" I still want to cry when I think about it. He told me the name of a town in Kansas. He looked like an old hippy. He was a small man, and didn't seem threatening at all. I was still scared to death.

"I am going to Kansas City," I told him. "I can take you that far."

He asked me if I was sure, of course, because I was doing something absolutely crazy. I told him I was and to throw his pack in the back seat and get in. He did. He buckled up as I started down the ramp, heart in my throat.

I said, "I hope you don't mind if I speed a little bit, I'm going to see my new grandson,"

"Oh," he says, "I still get high, too."

I didn't think it was possible but, my state of panic increased. I told him I meant driving over the speed limit and he chuckled and said it was okay with him. We did the small talk thing for the next several miles. He was going to a job his brother-in-law had for him. He had been down and out for a long time. He told me about the people who had helped him along the way. He talked a lot about his shoes and how bad they were and how he needed new shoes to do the new job.

When I looked at him, it was as if I were looking at a male me. He was my age, forty-seven. He was my size. He looked rough around the edges from a hard life, just like me. However, he was nice and non-threatening. Then, he asked me why I had stopped and picked him up. I said something like I had felt sorry for him because it was so cold out and I thought he had spent the night outside.

A few more miles down the road, he asked me that same question again. "Why did you pick me up?" This time, I felt a little bit uncomfortable as I joked that he was walking right in front of my SUV and I really had to either stop or hit him.

We drove and talked some more. The sun was up.

Then he asked me for a third time, "Why did you stop and pick me up?"

I couldn't believe that he had asked me the same question again. I looked at him and told him the truth, "You might think I am crazy but, I thought you might be Jesus, and I didn't want to take a chance on not stopping and picking you up, in case you *were* him." Oh my gosh, I was so choked up I could hardly speak those words. He just smiled at me.

As I write this, one of my favorite hymns comes to mind. I think of Him, in the road, ahead of me and I hear the words…. "Be not afraid. I go before you always."

It felt good to tell the truth about why I had

picked him up. Then he started telling me about the McDonald's in Bethany and how they had given him coffee for 20 cents the night before he slept outside in the cold and how this morning, they were going to charge him full price.

Then it hit me. "Are you hungry?"

His reply was, "Just a little."

We were almost in Kansas City by that time and I saw a junction up ahead with a McDonald's and a truck stop so I exited. Then the fear overcame me, again. I would have to get my purse out from where I had hidden it in order to pay for his food. My heart started pounding again as I wondered what would happen if he robbed me and I was left with no money or credit cards.

We were in the drive thru. He said he wanted a Big Mac, fries, and a coke. (my favorite) I ordered it, paid for it, gave it to him, then we got on the road again. I started to breathe easier when he asked me if I was hungry and offered me some of his food. I thanked him and said I was okay. I let out a sigh of relief. I hadn't been robbed, raped, or killed, yet.

My plan was to let him off after I got onto Interstate 70 in Independence, right by the Royals and Chiefs' stadiums. When we got close to the exit, he asked me, quite unexpected, to pull over.

I stopped on a concrete island. There were my three lanes, and two or three more exiting and some going the other direction, and lanes exiting on their side. It was crazy! It was the last place any person with a brain in his head would stop to let someone out. Panic, again!

He got out of the car and opened the back door

to get his pack. I was scared to get my purse out again, but I did. I handed him $40.00. He said he didn't want it but, I insisted. I told him I didn't want to think about him being hungry or sleeping outside again. Reluctantly, he took my two $20 bills.

I was somewhat mortified to be dropping anyone off in the middle of all that concrete and traffic. He thanked me and I drove into traffic again and started to get ready for my exit.

I looked in my rear view mirror, wondering where on earth he was going to go in order to not get run over, and, he was nowhere to be seen. It was as if he had disappeared.

I turned around and looked for him. There was no one, there. At that instant, it felt, as it had once before, as if the flood gates were opened and I was being showered with graces and love. I cannot tell you in words, what that was like.

I had been given another chance, and I was so thankful for it. I felt as though I would explode with joy and tears and gratefulness. I've never experienced such love. I felt like Mary Magdalene when she met Jesus after He had risen from the grave. I felt like the men on the road to Emmaus.

I drove on in a state of ecstasy. It would really take me a few weeks to absorb everything I had just experienced. However, almost immediately, I thought about Matthew 25:35-36, *for I was hungry and you gave me food, I was thirsty and you gave me drink, I was a stranger and you welcomed me, I was naked and you clothed me, I was sick and you visited me, I was in prison and you came to me.*

I started judging how I had done this time

around. I hate to even tell you this stuff but, I wouldn't be telling the truth if I didn't. I went down my checklist from the Bible. I had welcomed Him. I had given Him food and drink. However, I hadn't clothed Him! I realized instantly that I had a pair of brand new Nike tennis shoes in the back and they looked like men's shoes. I know they would have fit Him. He had spent so much time talking about shoes and His need for a good pair. What was wrong with me? Why hadn't I offered Him those shoes? My joy turned into regret. I judged that I had done a whole lot better than the last two times Jesus had come to see me, however, I still could have done more. I should have done better. I beat myself up all the way to my son's house.

twenty

My first-born grandson was perfect. He was like a little cupid, so chubby and cute. My first-born granddaughter sat so close to me while I held him. My first-born son was turning into a good man and father. I was happy and proud. I remembered holding him for the first time as I now held his son for the first time. Life was good. I was so exhausted after my trip that I don't know how much help I was to anyone. They really seemed to have everything under control, so I went to sleep. I spent the next day and then, I really started getting the feeling Katie needed me. I decided to take off and drive through the night again so I could be home when she woke up the next morning.

As I drove in the darkness, I noticed the full moon outside my driver's window. It stayed with me all the way home. I was still trying to take the experience with the hitchhiker in. Why had He asked me three times why I picked Him up? What would have happened if I hadn't finally told Him the truth? Why was He so much like me? Where had He gone after I dropped Him off?

As I got to Kansas City and passed the place where He had asked me to pull over, I couldn't believe I really had stopped there and let Him out. As I got to the place in Bethany where I had picked Him up, I thought I should make a little Shrine there the next time I came that way. Then I realized I should probably make Shrines at the other two places where I had met Him before. Then, I realized the entire world should be a Shrine to Our Lord as we meet Him in every single person we encounter. It seemed as if I understood a very deep truth. Everything in this life is a test and an encounter with Christ.

It dawned on me that Bethany was where Jesus' friends, Lazarus, Mary and Martha had lived. Why had He met me in Bethany? Did He consider me a friend? How long had He been orchestrating this lesson for me? I was convinced He had influenced Steve. Had He influenced the conception of my grandson to make the timing of his birth at a time when the girls were in school? There was so much to ponder. It would take me months before I had absorbed enough to be able to talk about any of it with other people. It would be over a year and a half before I would tell my husband. I did make it home though, in time to wake the girls up and take them to school.

twenty-one

My preparations for coming into the church were moving right along. I had finished reading *A Course in Miracles* for the second time. I was starting to talk more about my conversion and I had even joined a prayer group with some women from the church. I hardly knew who I was, anymore. I had changed so much. I liked to compare myself to St. Paul. I was blind but now I see.

One day, I had the thought that I wasn't like St. Paul at all. I was like St. Thomas. I would have never believed if I hadn't seen and felt. Then I found out it was the Feast Day of St. Thomas. Amazing! Day after day, lesson after lesson, I was learning more than I had learned in my entire life. I was getting so eager to receive Jesus in the Sacrament of the Eucharist that I could hardly contain myself.

I remember after I understood the Eucharist, they taught us in RCIA that Jesus was present in the tabernacles of every Catholic Church in the world.

For months, I had gone to the Adoration Chapel and thought it was only a place to pray. Then when I learned about Him being in the tabernacles, I would sit in the Chapel and wonder why they had Him over in the corner in that little tabernacle instead of on the Altar with the candles in the front of the Chapel. I'll never forget the day someone explained to me the monstrance in the middle of the candles on the Altar in the Chapel contained the Eucharist.

I felt so stupid. I had sat there for months, right in front of Him, and hadn't even known it. He had come into my living room, and basically tapped me on the shoulder and said, "Come here." And I had gone straight to Him not knowing what I was doing. Humiliated and humbled, I realized even though I thought I was learning a lot, I didn't know much. I still don't.

One thing I did know was that I wanted everybody I knew to experience what I had. I tried to get my husband to read my book, but he didn't like it and didn't think it made sense. I tried to read things out of it to my little old friend and she couldn't get it. I bought so many copies of that book and gave it to so many people but not one of them liked it or wanted to read it. I was disappointed. I just knew if they would keep on reading, they could hear Jesus talking to them as I had. I bought a Spanish version for a friend. I bought a Chinese version for another girl. I sent my mom a copy. That didn't go well. She started screaming to me that it was blasphemy and said she burnt it. People began telling me it was New Age. I researched what New Age was and found out it was nothing like New

Age.

New Age is not about Jesus. It is about energy and the center of the universal power of something. My book was written by Jesus. He talked to me in it. He talked about His cross and explained what He meant in the Bible when He said this or that. I went to the priest I had talked to before about lying to Courtney, and I told him about the book that had gotten me to where I was in my faith journey.

He asked me a simple question. "Has this book brought you closer to Jesus?"

I said, "Yes."

He said, "Well then, its good." End of discussion. I still wanted other people to have what I had but, I quit trying to push my book on them.

I realized Jesus had called Peter to repentance after he denied our Lord three times with the crowing of a cock. If He could cause Peter to repent with a rooster, He could call me to repentance with a book, which He had. He can and does use everything for good. I still wanted other people to have what I had, though.

I talked to another priest and told him I needed a book that would make my sons believe and want to be baptized. He laughed and told me he needed a book like that for some of his friends, too. He said the book that had done it for him was *Confessions* by St. Augustine. I read it. I didn't think it would work for my boys but I sent it to one, anyway.

I started reading my Course again for the third time but, I started reading other things, too. I read book after book. I had an insatiable appetite to learn. One of my favorite memories about reading my Course came on Saturday morning of the Easter Vigil, when I would become Catholic and receive Jesus in the Eucharist. There wasn't a mass that morning. Jesus wasn't in the Adoration Chapel, either.

The RCIA people had met for some scripture reading and then I had gone to the Chapel to read and pray. I remember that I just decided to open the book to wherever it opened and read. I loved every bit of it anyway. When I opened it up and looked down, the words that I saw were…. *On this day, you will be with me in Paradise.* Tears flowed. I was so happy to be where Jesus wanted me to be. As I was walking out of the Chapel, the lady that did Adoration before me was walking in.

She was always at the Chapel, it seemed. She had been so surprised when I had told her I wasn't Catholic back when I started doing the hour. She knew I was coming into the Church that night and she knew what it meant to me. We had become friends so, I stopped for a minute and told her I had gone in to pray about receiving Our Lord for the first time and He had told me that on this day, I would be in Paradise with him. She would tell me later, that she was putting together a Eucharistic Congress for the Cathedral of St. Paul and she was about to quit when I told her that.

She immediately changed her mind about quitting and went on to put together an amazing Congress for Our Lord. Jesus had used me to talk to her and he had used her to talk to me once, too. I was thinking about stopping my hour as it left me so tired most of the time. I was trying to decide what to do when I went to the Chapel one morning at 3:30.

She had turned around and said to me, "Never quit this hour. It is the most important thing you will ever do and it will change your life."

I smiled and thought, *where did that come from?* But, I knew where it had come from.

twenty-two

i had a dream one night. In my dream, I was working in an office and I was with a group of people gathered around a water fountain listening to a man talk. He was telling us what had happened to him the night before. He said he had gone with a friend to meet Jesus. He was excited as he told us about how amazing it was. He said he had never in his life experienced anything like it. Jesus was healing people. He said he saw miracles right before his eyes. He tried to explain how peaceful he felt but it was hard to describe because it was like nothing else he had ever experienced. He went on and on about it and then he said he was definitely going back after work and asked if anyone wanted to go with him. I said I wanted to.

We met after work and started walking to where Jesus was. He was in a hurry to get back. We were going very fast, almost running. We were in a city and he was holding my hand as we hurried down the street with him in front of me, pulling me along. We turned after a couple of blocks and turned again at the next corner.

Then it seemed as if we were in a maze. He took me through an alley to the next corner and then down another alley and another. We were going so fast and making so many turns. It felt as if I was in a huge market place in foreign country. One thing that I knew for sure after we got there, was that there was no way I would have ever found the place where Jesus was, by myself.

We were in a big space and there were many people there already but, Jesus saw us come in and smiled. It was amazing and I immediately knew why my friend had been so excited and in such a hurry to get back. We saw people be cured of every imaginable illness with just a look or touch of His hand. His voice was the most beautiful I had ever heard and the words coming out of His mouth were heavenly. Every time I looked at Him, He was always looking at me. It was too much to take in and I never wanted to leave. We did have to leave, eventually, and as we walked away, I could feel Him watching us. I turned and looked into His eyes and I felt like He was saying, "When are you going to come back and who are you going to bring with you?" I knew He would be looking and waiting for me until I returned.

My dream continued and it was the next day at work and this time, I was the one telling everybody about meeting Jesus and how my life would never be the same. Then it was me, taking someone to meet Him after work. This time was different, though. It was as if we were in a huge hospital. We were going down halls and turning and going up stairs and turning. It was very much like the first time, in as much as, we were going very fast and there was absolutely no way this person could have found where we were going if I hadn't been showing him the way.

I felt as if we were in a maze forever until we finally arrived. Instead of being in a big open space, this time we were in a big room. Jesus wasn't standing in a group of people like before. He was sitting on what looked like a gurney and covered with a white sheet. It made me think of how He is now on the Altar, in the Eucharist. Everything else was the same as before, though. People were healed. There were tears of joy on everyone's faces. Like before, every time I looked at Him, He was looking at me. He made you feel as if you were the only person there. Unfortunately, the time came for us to leave and it was just like before. He looked at you with eyes that said, "When are you coming back and who are you going to bring with you next time?" I knew in my heart that He was going to miss me until I returned.

My dream was over. It took days for it to all to sink in. What did it mean? I pondered it for a long time. I tried to tell my husband about it but I couldn't articulate it. It was too soon. Now, a few years later, I do think I fully understand it. I believe He was showing me that no one else would ever have the same experience as I did. I could quit buying books and giving them to people and quit thinking that if they did this or that, they would surely find Him, as I had. I am sure now that there are as many different paths to God as there are people. No two of us will ever know Him, or come to know Him, in exactly the same way.

I believe what the dream showed me was that the only effective way for any of us to evangelize is to simply tell people what has happened to us since we met Jesus and how He has changed our lives. Our honesty, our joy, and our excitement are all it takes for someone to want to see Him for themselves.

When they see what Jesus has done for us, they will know it's true. Then, He takes care of the rest. That is the reason I have written this book. I want you to know He is alive. He came into my living room and proved it to me.

You can experience Him in your life right now, wherever you are! I want you to understand God has placed each one of us here, on our own unique path. All we have to do is seek Him and we will find Him. Our purpose on this earth is to find our way home and to help others find their way, too. God Bless you, and thank you for letting me share my story with you.

twenty-three

i decided to end my story with the dream, although, my adventure in faith and my walk with Jesus and His mother are ongoing. There are a few little after thoughts I would like to share. You know how I told you my husband started going to church after he met me, which I hated. Now, I figured out we were married on the Feast of the Immaculate Heart of Mary, and our wedding song was *Into the Mystic* by Van Morrison.

When we made the headstone for our little girl's grave, we had a Rosary put on it, not knowing what it was. Our Blessed Mother showed me a picture of me when I was alone and so desperate after my baby died. I had picked up my father-in-law's rosary beads and tried to memorize the Hail Mary on our bed. I sat with my legs crossed and hands in the yoga position, wanting to memorize it so I could chant it and meditate to feel better.

I couldn't remember it from one time to the next and eventually gave up but, she let me know it was then, at that very instant, that she took me under her mantle and personally led me to her Son. We moved into our house on August 15, which is the Feast of the Assumption.

My conversion experience, when Jesus came into my living room and said, *"I am here."* was on August 6, the Feast of the Transfiguration.

When I looked at Courtney's new birth certificate that we got after the adoption, the date on it was September 13, the day my Hannah Leigh was stillborn. I believe if there are no coincidences, all of these things were orchestrated to help this little lost lamb find her way home. And, I am so grateful.

When we moved into the cabin on the lake, and I hated everybody I met, it was because of me, not them. I do not remember where I read this story but it was speaking directly of me. A man was working at a gas station when a person came in and said he was moving into town and asked what the people were like.

The attendant asked him what they were like where he lived now. He said they were the meanest, backstabbers and liars he had ever met. He told him he was afraid he would find the people in the new town pretty much the same as the old.

Then another guy came in and asked the same question. Again, the attendant asked what the people were like where he came from. The new person told him they were the nicest people in the world and they would do anything for anybody. The attendant told him he would find the people in this town very much the same. What we see on the outside is a reflection of what we have on the inside. Liars think everybody is lying to them. Thieves think people are going to steal from them. Cheaters don't trust people. I understand exactly what Jesus meant when He told us to take the plank out of our own eye before we try to take the sliver out of anyone else's. You see, that removes it from both.

When my dad was dying, I asked him if he would send me a couple of blessings from Heaven someday. He said he would. The first year after his death, I was having a really hard time and found myself crying at weird times, for no apparent reason. The Feast of the Visitation fell on what would have been my dad's birthday that year.

I found myself in a downpour when I spotted a petite lady, out in the rain. I was at a stop sign when I heard… *Give her your umbrella*. I thought, I can't because my girls will get all wet then. A second time I heard… *Give her your umbrella*. I thought, it's not mine to give, it's my husband's. Then a third time…*Give her your umbrella*. I rolled down the window and handed the umbrella to her in the pouring rain. She asked me if I was sure (sounds familiar) and I told her yes. The most beautiful face I've ever seen came to my window and said, "Bless you. Bless you. Jesus loves you and so do I." *Thank you Dad, and thank you Blessed Mother*.

My old lady friend has gone home to Our Lord now but, not before she finally told me what everybody had done to her that was so terrible. I found out they hadn't really done anything that mean to her at all. She had just decided to be offended. She realized it and I truly believe she was able to let go of it. And the young girl that had said what she said didn't make sense, well, she and her children lived with us for nine months and I learned that every time she said something didn't make sense, what she meant was, "I don't understand it." My friend was also able to understand that and she stopped being mad at her, too, and also me, for letting her move in.

One day I was skimming through the headlines on Spirit Daily and I saw one that said *Tennis Champion Becomes Nun.* I knew immediately that it had to Andrea Jaeger. Sure enough, it was her.

Lastly, I just want to tell you a little bit more about the hitchhiker story. I lamented not offering Him my shoes, every time I told anyone that story. I would go over it for days. One day, as I was beating myself up for not offering those Nikes, I heard His voice, almost scolding me.

"The reason you didn't offer him those shoes is because I didn't inspire you to offer him the shoes."

That shut me up real quick. I came to understand that every single thing in the world we do that is good, whether it be a smile or an offer of help, comes from Jesus. Everything else is us. God is good and we are not. I have tried to remember that ever since that day. I once tried to read *The Little Flowers of St. Francis.* I couldn't understand why he spent so much time putting himself down, and talking about how terrible he was, until I heard those words from Jesus. I get it now, St. Francis, I really do. Let this be our daily prayer... Inspire us O, Lord. Amen. Now, get out there and share your story!

about the author

Bev Diemler is a wife, mother, grandmother, and foster parent. She is a Missouri girl that's been living in Minnesota for eleven years. She used to think that her family was transferred because of work. She now will tell you that Providence brought them here, so she could *Be still and know that He is God.* Although she still dreams of going back home someday, her true desire is to spend the rest of her life making Jesus Christ known and loved.

Made in the USA
Monee, IL
05 December 2023

48244720R00075